ADO 2

Birds in the Sky

by Lucy and John Hawkinson

CHILDRENS PRESS, CHICAGO

I love to watch the flying birds . . .
Gulls that wheel and dip over the
cold, cold waves,

Library of Congress Catalog Card Number: 65-20888

Copyright © 1965, Children Press
All rights reserved. Printed in the U.S.A.
Published simultaneously in Canada
10 11 12 13 14 15 16 17 18 19 20 21 22 23 24 25 R 75

a pair of doves that fly like arrows
through the air,

or a flock of redwings chattering and swirling
in a red evening sky.

Ducks are swift and sure.
They beat their wings fast
as they rise and turn,
silhouetted against the sky.
Then down to the pond they go,
to land together
with a single splash.

With the fresh green leaves of spring, the warblers come.
Their flashing colors are all around, as they flit
from branch to branch.

And in the summer when the sun begins to set,
I love to watch the nighthawks in the sky.
They fly high, then suddenly make a breath-taking
dive, and then swoop up again.

On a dusty roadside
a little flock
of goldfinches
darts up in flashes
of gold and black.

And over the field,
a sparrow hawk
flutters in mid-air,
then drops like a shot
to the grass.

The empty sky is suddenly filled with swallows
darting about, gliding, diving, swiftly and gracefully.
When they swoop low just over my head, I can see
their bright, shiny colors. But high in the air,
they are all dark against the sky.

Then, just as suddenly
as they came, they seem
to disappear, and the sky
is quiet and empty again.

In May the terns come
to visit for a while.
They have a bouncy
kind of flight, and
their eyes are always
glued to the water below.
All of a sudden
they will fold their
long, slender wings and
dive straight down
into the water to
catch a little fish.

The great blue heron
has a long, lazy
beat of wings as he
glides over the still pond.

How funny he looks
trying to land, with his
wings flapping madly
and his legs outstretched
as he reaches for a limb
to balance on.

Cedar waxwings fly along
in a tight little group,
their wings beating
in unison. They alight
in the top of a tree
to chatter and rest,
and then off they go again.

I love to be in the quiet of a deep forest and see
a thrush. He zips through the trees never touching
a twig or rustling a leaf.

Happy little chimney swifts
chase about in the blue sky,
like children on a playground.
They wheel and dive and
zigzag, and seem to have
a wonderful time.

Sandpipers run on the beach in front of me.
Then up they go with a startled peep-peep
as they fly low over the water and circle
around behind me.

Bobwhites explode from the grass at my feet, whir off in all directions, and then join each other in the air.

High in the bright October sky, a flock of geese
fly south. Their necks are outstretched. Their
wings beat slowly. I can hear them honking
if it is quiet.

I watch them fly until they are tiny specks in the sky,
and it makes me glad just to be here watching them.

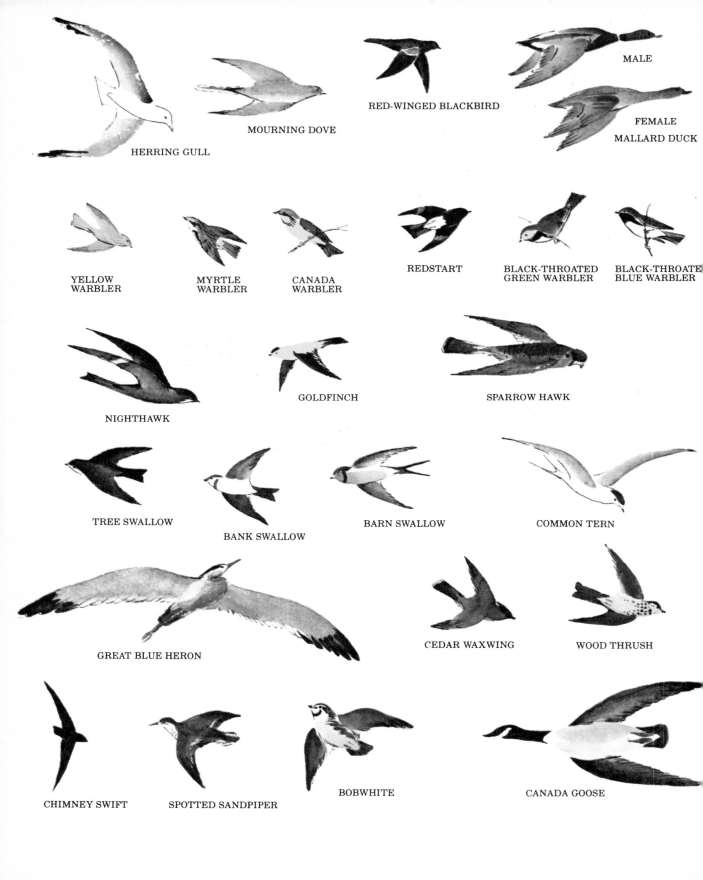

HERRING GULL

MOURNING DOVE

RED-WINGED BLACKBIRD

MALE

FEMALE
MALLARD DUCK

YELLOW
WARBLER

MYRTLE
WARBLER

CANADA
WARBLER

REDSTART

BLACK-THROATED
GREEN WARBLER

BLACK-THROATED
BLUE WARBLER

NIGHTHAWK

GOLDFINCH

SPARROW HAWK

TREE SWALLOW

BANK SWALLOW

BARN SWALLOW

COMMON TERN

GREAT BLUE HERON

CEDAR WAXWING

WOOD THRUSH

CHIMNEY SWIFT

SPOTTED SANDPIPER

BOBWHITE

CANADA GOOSE